5 -03

9/03
∅

READING POWER

American Tycoons

John Jacob Astor

and the Fur Trade

Lewis K. Parker

The Rosen Publishing Group's
PowerKids Press™
New York

Published in 2003 by The Rosen Publishing Group, Inc.
29 East 21st Street, New York, NY 10010

First Edition

Book Design: Daniel Hosek

Photo Credits: Cover © National Portrait Gallery, Smithsonian Institution/ Art Resource; pp. 4–5, 17, 18–19 General Research Division, The New York Public Library, Astor, Lenox and Tilden Foundations; pp. 5 (inset), 20 (top) © AP/Wide World Photos; p. 6 © Erich Lessing/Art Resource; pp. 7, 20 (bottom) Print Collection, Miriam and Ira D. Wallach Division of Art, Prints and Photographs, The New York Public Library, Astor, Lenox and Tilden Foundations; p. 8 R.A. Blakelock (1847–1919) *Fifth Avenue and Eighty-ninth Street 1868*, 1868, oil on canvas, Gift of Archer M. Huntington, 32.333, courtesy Museum of the City of New York; p. 9 © Charles E. Rotkin/Corbis; p. 10 (inset) © Christie's Images/Corbis; pp. 10–11 Dan Hosek; pp. 12–13 © Hulton/Archive/Getty Images; p. 13 (inset) © MapArt; pp. 14–15 © Giraudon/Art Resource; p. 19 (inset) © Corbis; p. 21 © Oscar White/Corbis

Library of Congress Cataloging-in-Publication Data

Parker, Lewis K.
John Jacob Astor and the fur trade / Lewis K. Parker.
    p. cm. — (American tycoons)
Summary: Introduces John Jacob Astor, who came to the United States in 1784, began work as a clerk for a fur trader, later went into business for himself, and died in 1848 as the richest man in America.
Includes bibliographical references and index.
ISBN 0-8239-6447-7 (lib. bdg.)
1. Astor, John Jacob, 1763-1848—Juvenile literature. 2. Businesspeople—United States—Biography—Juvenile literature. [1. Astor, John Jacob, 1763-1848. 2. Businesspeople.] I. Title.
CT275.A85 P29 2003
380.1'092—dc21

2002000087

Contents

Coming to America

The fur trade and real estate in New York City made John Jacob Astor one of the richest tycoons in American history. John Jacob Astor was born on July 17, 1763, in Waldorf, Germany. He was one of twelve children. His family was very poor. Astor left home at sixteen to work for his brother, making musical instruments in England. In 1783, he went to America.

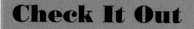

Check It Out

Astor had seven flutes to sell and about $25 when he arrived in America.

Astor worked hard throughout his life to make his fortune.

Waldorf, Germany, in 1768.

Early Life in America

In New York City, Astor worked as a clerk for a fur trader. In 1785, he married Sarah Todd. They had five children.

Astor opened his own store one year later. He sold musical instruments and traded furs. Astor quickly became successful.

Astor's business became successful because many people liked to wear fur hats and coats.

"The man who makes it the habit of his life to go to bed at nine o'clock usually gets rich and is always reliable...good habits in America make any man rich."
—John Jacob Astor

Sarah Todd was a good businesswoman. While Astor was away on trips, she ran the business.

Astor used the profits from his business to buy land. He bought a lot of land north of the city limits of New York City. Later, the property was worth much more than he paid for it.

Most of the land that Astor bought north of New York City was farmland with small houses.

Check It Out

In 1803, Astor paid $25,000 for 70 acres north of New York City. By the 1870s, the land was worth $20 million! Today, this area is called Times Square, which is now a part of New York City.

The Fur Trade

In 1800, Astor bought ships and began sailing to China to sell furs. He was one of the first American businessmen to trade there. Astor made a lot of money on his trips to China. He sold the furs and bought tea. Then he sold the tea in America.

Russia

China

Astor used ships like this one to take furs from New York City to China.

Australia

On each trip to China, Astor made about $50,000.

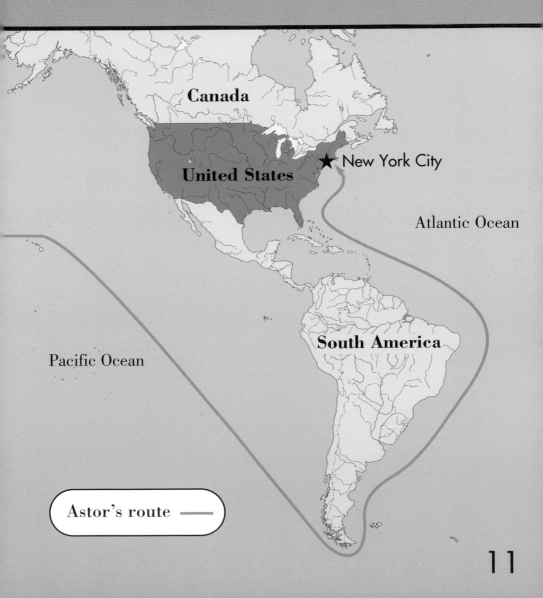

Canada

United States

★ New York City

Atlantic Ocean

South America

Pacific Ocean

Astor's route ——

In 1808, Astor started the American Fur Company. By this time, America had expanded west of the Mississippi River. Astor wanted to set up trading posts in the West to buy furs. He formed the Pacific Fur Company in the Northwest. Then, he built a trading post called Fort Astor on the Columbia River.

Fort Astor is now the city of Astoria, Oregon.

Fort Astor was built in 1811.

Many American ships were attacked by England during the War of 1812.

Astor's plans for fur trading in the West failed. During the War of 1812 between the United States and England, one of his ships exploded. Then the English took over Fort Astor. Soon, the Pacific Fur Company went out of business.

Astor didn't build much on the land he owned. Instead, he rented the land to others.

However, Astor did give $850,000 to people in Waldorf, Germany, to build the Astor House. It was a special school for poor children. It was also a place where the elderly and needy could go for help.

In his will, Astor left $400,000 to start the Astor Library. It is now a part of the New York Public Library in New York City.

The Astor House helped many people in the town where Astor was born.

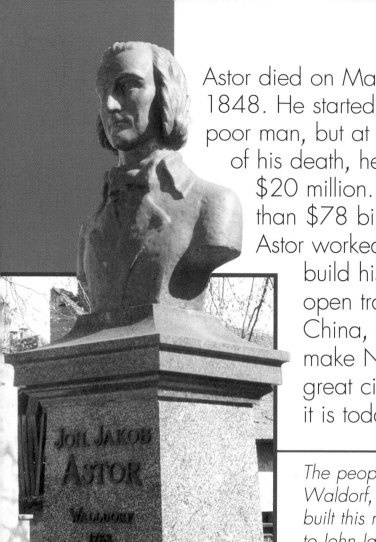

Astor died on March 29, 1848. He started out as a poor man, but at the time of his death, he was worth $20 million. That is more than $78 billion today! Astor worked hard to build his fortune, open trade with China, and help to make New York the great city it is today.

Joh. Jakob
Astor
Waldorf
1763

The people of Waldorf, Germany, built this monument to John Jacob Astor.

Time Line

July 17, 1763	1783	1785
John Jacob Astor is born in Germany	Went to America	Marries Sarah Todd

Astor's son, William B. Astor, purchased even more property for the family. He also built more than 700 stores and apartment buildings in New York City.

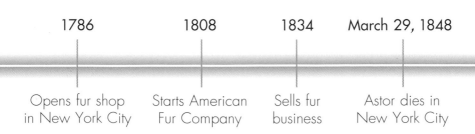

1786	1808	1834	March 29, 1848
Opens fur shop in New York City	Starts American Fur Company	Sells fur business	Astor dies in New York City

Glossary

businessmen (**bihz**-nihs-mehn) men who work for
  or run companies

elderly (**ehl**-duhr-lee) old people

expanded (ehk-**spand**-ehd) having become larger

income tax (**ihn**-kuhm **taks**) money that is taken from
  people's earnings to support the government

musical instruments (**myoo**-zuh-kuhl **ihn**-struh-muhnts) tools
  used to make music

profits (**prahf**-ihts) the money a business person has left
  after the bills and salaries are paid

real estate (**reel** eh-**stayt**) buildings and land

rented (**rehnt**-ehd) letting someone pay money to
  use property

trading posts (**trayd**-ihng **pohsts**) places where goods
  are bought, sold, and traded

tycoons (ty-**koonz**) businesspeople with a lot of wealth
  and power

will (**wihl**) a legal paper that states a person's wishes for
  what to do with his or her money and belongings
  after death

Resources

Books

*America in the Time of
Lewis and Clark: 1801–1850*
by Sally Senzell Isaacs
Heinemann Library (2001)

A Frontier Fort on the Oregon Trail
by Scott Steedman
Peter Bedrick Books (1994)

Web Sites

Due to the changing nature of Internet links, PowerKids Press has developed an on-line list of Web sites related to the subjects of this book. This site is updated regularly. Please use this link to access the list:

http://www.powerkidslinks.com/aty/jja/

Index

Word Count: 497

Note to Librarians, Teachers, and Parents

If reading is a challenge, Reading Power is a solution! Reading Power is perfect for readers who want high-interest subject matter at an accessible reading level. These fact-filled, photo-illustrated books are designed for readers who want straightforward vocabulary, engaging topics, and a manageable reading experience. With clear picture/text correspondence, leveled Reading Power books put the reader in charge. Now readers have the power to get the information they want and the skills they need in a user-friendly format.